For

Support

Never Let Yourself Go: With or Without Him

—Author—

A Reid

July 2016

Angela Reid

—Never Sweat (chase) a MAN —

Never Let Yourself Go—With or Without Him.

First Printing December 2012

ISBN: 978-1-4675-4042-1

Never Let Yourself Go – With or Without Him
Angela Reid Enterprises
(313) 384-9556
msauthoress@yahoo.com
www.neverletyourselfgo.com

Cover design by Duane Johnson of Legwork Graphics
Edited by Deanna Smith, Sue Pauling, and Gloria Palmer

Table of Contents

Introduction

After reading *Never Let Yourself Go*, the reader will learn to:

- Love yourself fully

- Never chase or sweat ANY man, even if you like him

- Maintain the best appearance, especially in public

- Have a meaningful life that defines you

- Stroke a man's ego

- Screen a man

- Duty Date 101

- Be appreciated in a relationship with a man

- Know when to call a man

- Let a man be a man

- Negotiate intimacy

- Pull the sex plug if need be

Foreword

I am Angela Reid. I was born and raised in Detroit, Michigan. I have three children and one grandchild. I've been married twice. Life is funny. You wish you knew then what you know now. I have always been an independent and giving person.

Since I was about ten years old, I wanted to grow up and make things right in the world! Of course, this feat is impossible for any human. However, as an attempt, I'd like this book to be considered as one of my contributions to this well-needed change. Its purpose is to reach out to women, younger and older, with the message to never let yourself go—with or without him!

I've had many life experiences, which have brought me to the point of writing this influential book. I want to reach out to women and young girls by relaying my story on love and relationships. Although my first marriage lasted only five years, I *was* a young mother, and I was in love. He actually was my first love. I met my second husband in 1989. We started out as friends, and I'm sure that's why we were together for twenty years.

My message to women, and I stress this wholeheartedly, is NEVER lose or let yourself go—with or without a man. There were, and still are, many lessons for me to learn. In fact, I'm forever learning! One thing is for sure, you should learn from your mistakes so that you don't repeat them.

Again, my goal is to help women keep it together, whether you're in love or not. You can be in love with a man and still be strong, happy, and maintain your beauty, and vice versa. In fact, when in love, one should possess a special glow, perhaps the glow of love, since the closest thing to God is love. You can't go wrong with that.

My mission is to give advice on how to keep high self-esteem at all times. Remember, if you don't think highly of yourself, no one else will. Learn to love yourself, with or without a man. Never let yourself go . . . with or without him!

D E D I C A T I O N

I dedicate this book

to myself,

my two sisters,

and all the females I hope to reach.

Chapter 1: Love Yourself (No Matter What)

Loving yourself is easy. There is only one you, and you only have one life to live. It makes perfect sense to live while loving yourself. The most important part of life is to take care of yourself by eating healthy, staying fit through exercise, and maintaining mental stability by way of meditation and prayer. These three functions are pertinent to a happy and fulfilling life. Determination, contentment, and attitude will lead to unbelievable heights.

You are in control of your feelings. Smile when you don't feel like it. Laugh when it's easier to cry. Love even if it feels like nobody else loves you. Take an inventory of your life and its possessions. Be grateful for what you have. If you are not satisfied, you and only you can change what you have for the better. Try it. Believe me, it works. I do it every day. In fact, I dare you.

Remember your first love, and how you were willing to go the extra mile just to preserve the sensation of that emotion? Well, somehow you must find a way to duplicate that same passion for yourself. Love yourself at all costs—you are worth it because you are somebody!

You are a salesperson, and the person on sale is you. You are selling yourself every day. The question is, do you love the product that is on display? Impress yourself first; then you will impress others. Root for yourself; love yourself.

Angela Reid

"What do you think about you?

How do you feel about you?

Other people treat you like you treat yourself.

You cannot really be mistreated unless

somewhere in your mind, you mistreat yourself.

Be good to you."

— Rev Run
Words of Wisdom:
Daily Affirmations of Faith

Chapter 2:
Look Good
(At All Times)

Make an extra effort to look your best morning, noon, and night. Take pride in your appearance. Sometimes things happen in our lives that have a negative effect and, in turn, make us feel terrible. But that doesn't mean we should allow the internal to change the external. Be sure to work out the problem that's causing the troubles, but "never let 'em see ya' sweat," so to speak. From my personal experiences in dealing with people, you should always try to look good, no matter what side of the bed you wake up on.

For example, I went to the dentist in pain from a toothache, and I still had my best look on, to the point the dentist was flirting with me. I was so flattered, even while in pain. So, ladies, please keep your best look on at all times. You're worth it; looking good plays a role in your self-esteem and confidence.

Another example: I had a co-worker who didn't care how she looked—until she found herself attracted to a man. She began to come to work with makeup on, wearing her hair in different ways, and wearing more seductive clothing—all to get the attention of this man. If she had felt that way about herself all along, he would have noticed her before she noticed him. So please, ladies, look good at all times.

Your outward appearance produces a certain level of respect. Carry yourself like a lady and you will be treated like a lady. Plus, you never know whom you may meet on any given day. If you are feeling your worst and your appearance matches, it may be difficult for Mr. Right to spot you from across a crowded room.

We all have bad-hair days. But unless you're trying to make a fashion statement, don't go out with rollers in your hair. And please, no pajamas, slippers, or house shoes outside of your home. This type of wear is for indoors. You should care about your appearance! Image is everything!

Grooming is essential to loving yourself. When you look and smell good, it actually makes you feel a lot better. This is pertinent whether you have a man or not. I've seen some women who let their looks go down the drain after they get a man. Girl, please! Keep it together. You should wear clothing that's appropriate for whatever the occasion.

Listen to Mrs. Geraldine M.: "At age 52, I never wore makeup or did my nails. I was a dud. Angela inspired me to take time for myself and look good every day. After paying attention to how I looked, I began to love myself more and gained more self-confidence. Don't get me wrong; I'm not striving for approval, but we are very physical beings, and great opportunities can be missed simply because someone judged you on the strength of their first impression of your exterior. Keep your best look on at all times. You're worth it!"

Chapter 3: Have a Life (Your Own)

Never allow your life to revolve around somebody else's. You are an individual who must love you before you can love someone else. If this is a weakness that you possess, there are ways to focus on your livelihood instead.

Stay busy and try to accomplish everything you want out of life. I am a single mom who works a full-time job, attends school full-time, and now I am writing books. I have to find time for me. I am asked out on dates that I have to turn down because of my tight schedule. When I do fit in a date, my date always asks me when I have time to do anything. I tell him I work it out somehow.

It's easy, ladies, to have a life your own. By concentrating and trying to fulfill your own goals, there won't be time to worry about somebody else's. Never let a man think you don't have your own interests, plans, or goals. You must stay active by participating in a variety of activities. Volunteer, work out, shop, enroll in school, or go on a well-deserved vacation. Spend time with family and friends, go to the library or church or parties, read books, etc. Basically, force him to fit into your schedule. Ever heard the phrase, "Get in where you fit in?" Never allow a man to dictate your destiny.

Waking up to live another day proves there is a purpose to this crazy thing called life. You must take full advantage of every breathing second. Live it to the fullest and recognize your God-given blessings because they were set aside especially for you.

"Life is a stage and

We are actors in a play called life.

We write our own script and

Revise it as we please.

Who are you in this play?

Are you sad, broke, busted, or disgusted,

Or are you happy, wealthy, well dressed,

and vibrant?

It's up to you."

— Rev Run
Words of Wisdom:
Daily Affirmations of Faith

Chapter 4:
Never Sweat
(Chase)
A Man

Never, ever, sweat or chase a man. This type of behavior simply makes him run from you! He knows you're interested just by the communication you maintain. Please don't call and curse him out if he has stood you up. He knows he stood you up! Remember that sometimes silence is golden.

After being abandoned, don't call for anything. I am telling you from experience, he will call or text you. If you call, you are going to get his voicemail because he knows he left you high-and-dry. In essence, he probably needs time to get it together.

Most importantly, and to keep it real, he owes *you* the call because *he* stood *you* up. Keep doing you and, most of the time, he will call or text eventually. If he doesn't, oh well! Life goes on. I'm sure there are others who'd want to date you, so keep it cool. You have to stand firm and be strong.

If or when he calls, don't even mention his blunder. When he asks you how you're doing, tell him that you're just wonderful—because you ARE—and it will have him wondering if he has made a huge mistake! He will proceed to explain what happened without one question from you.

When he invites you out or wants to see you, it's okay to turn him down sometimes. Even if you like him a lot, just wait it out; then accept the next invitation. Don't even sweat it, because while you're waiting on the right man, the wrong ones are showing you exactly what a good man really looks like!

Take the risk of losing a man before you let him send you on an unnecessary mission. For example: One day when I was at work, there were two gentlemen waiting to make a purchase. One was complaining about a female who kept calling him over and over. He was telling his friend, "Man, she keeps calling me. Doesn't she see I'm not responding?" Eventually she left a voicemail, cursing him out. They were laughing and talking about her. So, ladies, please don't chase a man. There's no need to chase him because you're too preoccupied with the ones chasing you, period.

I once dated a gentleman who would call or text to see how I was doing because he wasn't hearing from me enough. I call and text a man who calls and texts me. I think that it's only good manners to respond to anyone who reaches out to you. If I don't hear from a man, I eventually delete his number from my phone. Let me tell you, ladies, every single man who I have deleted has always called or texted me back. It never fails. There's no reason to keep calling or texting a man who shows no interest in reciprocity; so keep it moving.

I have a girlfriend who lives in Chicago, Ms. Cece. I gave her the same advice, and she tried it with the men she was dating. She called me screaming, "Girl, I did what you said. I stopped calling and texting, and they began to call and text me, one by one at different times, complaining about not hearing from me!" She told every last one of them that she's just wonderful.

I have another girlfriend, Ms. T., who lives here in Michigan. She had been dating a man for three years and was suspicious that he was being unfaithful. Then she found phone numbers in his possession and cards addressed to him from other females, and he began to disrespect her. She broke up with him and took my advice not to sweat him—no calling, no texting. If she did text, it was dry or a one-word response. He couldn't handle that. He was calling and texting the whole time she and I were at lunch. You see, ladies, it works. You don't have to sweat or chase a man. Let him chase you!

One final example: I gave another girlfriend, Ms. L., the same advice—never sweat or chase a man. A gentleman she was seeing would tell her he was going to take her out or call her back, then would leave her high-and-dry. She would call me complaining that he didn't call or come take her out. I told her to cut off all communication with him, and she did. To her surprise, one week later he called. She was shocked. I had told her he would if she would be cool and silent. She really liked this gentleman. I told her it didn't matter if she loved him—don't chase or sweat him. She was satisfied with the results.

Again, ladies—NEVER sweat or chase a man, period. A gentleman told me straight up that he didn't like it at all when women chased him. In fact, he pursued who he wanted, and it wasn't any woman who had pursued him. Think about it, ladies. Don't send yourself through unnecessary hang-ups. It's not worth it.

Chapter 5:
The Screening
Process

You must, I repeat, you <u>must</u> take him through a screening process. You have to make sure you get somebody you truly want. Make sure he has your best interests at heart. He also has to have something to bring to the table. Make an extra effort to get to know the person of interest. Ask questions about his career goals, his transportation, his place, and most of all—his *state of mind*. Make sure he is *secure with himself.*

Again, please screen your potential man because you have to know what his real intentions are with you. Remember, you're wonderful, and you don't want to be worked over by a man who doesn't mean you any good. If he gets impatient and begins to pressure you for sex during your screening process, then more than likely he's not the one for you. You have to see what sacrifices he will make for you. Selfishness is not a trait you want the man you love to have. During the screening, his real and true colors will come out. This gives you an opportunity to choose him or deny him the opportunity to get to know you better.

We are all imperfect and we all sin. But, if this man lies to you about his name, occupation, past and present relationships, or even his criminal record, he's probably not the right choice in the first place. Without questioning him and getting to know him, you may get caught in a relationship, which is based on a lie, and was destined to fail from the start.

Remember, you don't have to answer to **any** man you're not married to. Even in a marriage, there's a level of respect to maintain without losing yourself or letting yourself go. So, ladies, please send them through the screening process.

Sometimes you may have to pull some tricks out of your sleeve to see if he is on the up-and-up. This is totally acceptable because you don't have time for heartache.

What sort of tricks? For example, call from your phone. If you don't get an answer, wait a few minutes then call him from your girlfriend's phone. If he answers, you will know that he is dodging you. Hang up; now you will know how to play him. Keep that secret to yourself. He doesn't have to know that you pulled that trick out of your sleeve.

Chapter 6:
Duty Date

Here you are, waiting on the right man, and learning life lessons with all of the wrong ones. Always date other men so you don't obsess over one. It will make it easy for you not to sweat a man. Go ahead, get wined and dined, because men are all different. Some are gentle, sweet, loving, and compassionate—real gentlemen.

Duty dating is keeping your options open and dating more than one man at a time. To find love, you have to open up your heart and risk being hurt. You have to step out on faith and go for it, of course with a high level of intelligence and common sense.

A life without love is nothing at all. I don't know about you, but I want someone to love, and I want someone to love me. Isn't that what everyone really wants? Therefore, you must date in order to know who's right for you. If you are looking for love, protect your heart, but also be open to the possibility of falling in love. As a quick note, duty dating can be with any nationality of men. Keep it interesting, with no limits.

Duty dating, to me, is giving yourself a chance to see that there are some good men out there who want to take you out; men who will respect you, honor you, open your car door, hold out your chair at dinner, let you order first, pay attention to you, etc.

I went on a date with a man who was Dominican and Sicilian. He was such a gentleman throughout the entire dinner. In fact, our date went so well that we were the last ones to leave the restaurant. When we did get ready to leave, it was raining outside. He wanted me to wait inside until he retrieved an umbrella so I wouldn't get wet. I told him that I was flattered and he didn't have to do that. He did take off his suit jacket and used it as an umbrella so I wouldn't get wet going to my car. I felt so special on that date. The next day, he sent me a beautiful text message with roses and a teddy bear attached. That was a date I'll always remember.

Another date I went on was with an Asian gentleman. He was an architect engineer. He was very intelligent. We dated the whole summer of 2008. What a nice, sweet, smart, respectful gentleman! We even had lunch in his corner office at his place of employment. He always called me; I never chased him at all.

To summarize duty dating, if you're looking for a man, give yourself a chance to see what all men are like. I have even had dates where I was ready to leave only ten minutes into the date.

On one particular date with an African American gentleman, we were having great conversation and getting along well, until he told me that I was a bit egotistical. I was shocked he felt that way, and I firmly told him that he was mistaking egotistical for the confidence I have in myself. Then I realized he was threatened by that, so I ended the date quickly.

So, you see, ladies, dating can be good. Duty date and the right man will come along. Never let a bad date stop you.

Chapter 7:
His Ego,
Stroke It

Every man loves it when you tell him how wonderful he is or how talented he is or how well-dressed he is or how good-looking he is. Tell him how proud you are of him and, please, praise him in front of other people. He will love it. Tell him when he does things that please you. Tell him how sweet he is. Call him little pet names like sweetie pie, boo, cutie pie, sweetheart, sweet darling, suga, etc. Believe me, it builds his faith in you and it secures him. It shows your strength as a woman and that you are secure with yourself. So go ahead and stroke his ego.

Sometimes when he is feeling down about something, or maybe there was a situation where he couldn't help or wasn't there when you needed him due to circumstances he couldn't control, your words of encouragement can uplift and smooth over a sticky situation. Don't put him down. It is okay to tell him that there's no love lost, and it will be all right. Just continue to let him know it will be okay. He will love you for it.

From my experience, every man loves it when you stroke his ego. For every man that has been in my life, I have had a pet name that I called him by—babe, sweetheart, darling, suga, suga bear, suga lump, etc.—in person, in text messages, voicemails, e-mails, or whatever, and I would get a positive response. One gentleman told me, "I love it when you call me darling." In fact, he would call me sweetheart, etc. Everyone wants to be cherished.

Chapter 8: You Gotta Let a Man Be a Man

There's nothing you can do but let a man be a man. His character can't be changed. He is what he is. Don't let it affect you in a bad way. If it continues to affect you adversely, then he's probably not the right man for you.

We as women must learn to control our emotions. You have to be secure with yourself first in order to be secure with a man because he is going to do what he wants to anyway. He has his own personal liberty, and you have yours. So, when he says he's going out with the guys, let him! If you follow my proven techniques, you can and will be successful with love, relationships, and even marriage. Just continue to **do you**. I promise you, it works.

Just remember that whatever his personality— it is **his**. Please don't let it change who **you** are; just let it be. If you don't like it, leave it alone and realize that sometimes when our hearts are in it, it's not that easy to just move on. But that too will pass. There are plenty more where he came from, and there's bound to be one for you. Don't let yourself get too attached early on in the relationship

For example, my daughter lives with her boyfriend. Early in their relationship, she complained about him going out on the town with his boys. I would tell her she had to get over that, and she should go out with her girlfriends sometime. It took her a while to get over it, but she eventually moved on from that part of their relationship to where they don't argue about him going out. Again, whatever a man's character is, it's his—just stand firm in who you are. Do you, and do it well.

There are some things about a man you love that you will put up with; just don't let yourself go in the process. Maintain your sanity, your dignity, your pride, your personality, your liberty, and your virtue as a woman. Keep your appearance and your confidence.

You can't change any man. That's why you have to stand firm and love you, look good, have or get a life, and live it to the fullest! Aim to become a blessing in his life, so that he doesn't forget the lady you are. Then he will always appreciate you. However, never sacrifice your happiness in the relationship!

Chapter 9:
You Gotta
Be a Woman
(At All Times)

Know your place as a woman and maintain your integrity. My mom always told me to be a lady no matter what relationship I was in. You have to give respect to get respect. If at any time you are not getting respect, you need to leave that person alone because you deserve to be respected, no matter what. The bottom line is this: Know your place as a woman in any relationship, and stand your ground. Never allow anyone to take your womanhood away from you!

A woman in a relationship sticks by her man, especially if he loves, appreciates, respects, and cherishes her and her opinions. What you don't want to be is a doormat for any man. Again, know your self-worth.

Be a woman of real beauty (a lady) who smiles through troubles, gathers strength through distress, and grows from lessons learned. Proceed in your relationship in this manner, and if the relationship ends . . . maintain your dignity and always be a lady.

Remember, strength is the key to success. Sometimes you have to let him know he was wrong, but of course, in a pleasant way. You don't have to bash or belittle him to make him aware. Be a mature woman and a lady about it as you come and go, and always remain in good spirits. You may want to curse him out; but, you're a lady, so don't do it. Simply be done because you don't need a man to curse out and bring added stress and negativity to your circle.

Relationships should consist of love, peace, and consideration of the other's feelings. Ladies, a good man will remember and respect that more than if you leave in a rage. Keep it grown and sexy. There is nothing sexy about a head spinning at a three-hundred-and-sixty-degree angle, eyes as red as fire, and horns growing out the sides of your head. That only resembles what TV portrays as a wicked demon or the devil himself! Women are more powerful than they know.

Chapter 10: Nothing to Lose

Always keep it real. Never make a fool out of yourself for any man. However, it is okay to let him know how you feel about him. In fact, it is silly to play games and not make him aware of your intentions. He should respect and cherish a woman who knows what she wants. If you have been seeing a man and you like him, it's okay to tell him. What do you have to lose?

These emotions come and go, but remember, you are in control of them. You can show him better than you can tell him. Send roses to his job or his house. This show of affection will catch his attention for sure. He will have no other choice but to know how you feel about him. Take it from me; it's something I love to do for a man. The results are explosive! Try it and see.

It's okay to express to him what you feel. These actions should encourage him and make it easier for him to reciprocate his feelings for you. If the feeling isn't mutual, you will know. Be woman enough to move on.

In 2001, I was in a relationship where I was feeling this gentleman, and we began to get really close. I wanted to show him how I felt, so I had a dozen red roses delivered to his place of employment. He told me that when the roses arrived, he had no idea they were for him because he worked in a large facility. When the delivery person walked up to him, he was so shocked and surprised! He called me immediately and thanked me profusely. I left such an impact on him that we still communicate to this day.

I surprised another gentleman I was dating with a single, long-stemmed red rose. I was going over to his apartment to spend the night with him. I showed up at the door with a trench coat on over a black teddy and high heels. I put the rose behind my back until he opened the door to greet me. Then I popped the rose out like, 'Here, baby, for you.' He, too, was surprised and shocked, but loved it. We also still keep in touch.

So, it's okay to show them how you feel with small gestures. They will never forget you.

Chapter 11: Make Sure He Appreciates You (Before Intimacy)

When you meet a man, you should expect to go out on the town. A "real" man *wants* to take you out and spend quality time. If his interest is beyond casual sex, he should be willing to find out who you are first. What better way to get to know a person than to go on a date?

Do not sleep with a man on or before the first date. Sex is a negotiation—NOT mandatory! There are always going to be highs and lows in dating, so never sleep with a man before he proves he's worthy of your most intimate and sacred display of love. There is a chance he may **never** take you out if he's already conquered the undeserved prize.

Believe me when I tell you, ladies, I've heard this right out of the horse's mouth. Males have made it clear time and time again that if a female gives it up quick and easy, there's no challenge or intrigue left. He also may have second thoughts about your promiscuity and worry about other suitors like him.

I have a platonic male friend, Mr. G. He told me that if a female sleeps with him before he has taken her even to McDonald's, he will never take her out because he already got what he wanted. He also said that he has had females who would require him to take them out.

So, ladies, please be aware. Men go the extra mile for those who require it. They will play you how you allow them to play you. Please take my advice and make sure he appreciates you before you negotiate intimacy. Give yourself time to figure out his real intentions. Know that you can get any man you want to have sex with, but what you want is one who will put a symbol of love on your finger—preferably diamonds, of course— before giving your all to him! Plus, it's too risky in this new age to have sex with just any random man who says that he likes you or you're pretty. You already know you're an attractive woman because you have already taken the advice of staying on point in the appearance department, right? His flattery is always nice, but he still needs to prove that he's worthy first.

Another thing to remember is a man falls in love with your virtue as a woman—not your body! Always remember that. Never give up sex thinking you're trapping him; then that's all it's going to be—sex. If that's all you want from him, then I guess it's okay. But if it's a man you want more from, then you need to negotiate to find out what he wants from you.

Please be careful! No random sex—unless that is all you want from him—and be sure to wrap it up. HIV and AIDS are real!

Chapter 12: Know When to Call

Ladies, as I said in chapter 4, never, ever, sweat or chase a man! If he has established a pattern of calling, texting, e-mailing, etc., then by all means call him, too, but not excessively! Perhaps leave a voice mail or even a text message, but like I said previously, never sweat him. He knows every time you call, and he knows when you are **not** calling.

In the beginning, space out when you initiate contact. If he doesn't call you, delete his number everywhere you have it! Even if you like him, he may not be into you, and if he's not into you, he's not into you—so don't sweat it. Duty date!

I have had men tell me that I'm acting like a stranger by not constantly making contact. They express how they have been waiting for my call, or I will get e-mails or text messages, all pertaining to the fact that they haven't heard from me. I always tell them I am wonderful and thinking of them.

You can reach out to them, and if you don't get an answer, leave a message or a text—just once! Even if you get a response a day later, it's okay; just don't chase him.

I know it is hard not to make contact when you have feelings for him. If he is into you, he will respond. Just you watch. You have to let him miss you. Stay strong and stay silent. If he is really feeling you, he will call or try to come see you somehow. ***Don't call him, especially if he isn't calling you***! You will get the urge to call—don't do it!

If I've had constant contact with a man who claimed he liked me or wanted to take me out or had taken me out, and we've kept the lines of communication open, but suddenly he isn't responding to my texts or returning phone calls within the week, I will cut off all communication. Every single time I have deleted any particular man, he has always, always resumed contact with me!

Mr. Rob, a Michigan state trooper, has had his number deleted several times. Every time he would call or text me, I would ask who he was. He would be offended because I didn't know it was him calling. I asked him if he was serious! How did he expect me to know who he was when there had been no communication between us? This proves that he knew I wasn't calling or texting him. I just kept it moving. I don't have time for games. The truth is, I liked him; I just wasn't going to chase him. I had forgotten about him and to my surprise, he showed up. You see, ladies, never sweat them. You don't need to.

Ms. Cece, a single mother of two boys, expressed to me that she wasn't happy with her son's father with whom she lived, so she and her sons had moved out. They went back to live at a property she owned, and she began to live her life without him. After cutting off all contact, she expressed how hard it was because she really loved him, but I told her he had to love, appreciate, and respect her.

Ms. Cece took my advice and didn't make contact for a week. Then he called her. She was so surprised. She called me screaming and hollering, saying he missed her, wanted her to come home, and wanted to know why she hadn't called or texted him. She was so excited, but she had already moved on. She was duty dating and didn't intend to go back. To this day, she has not gone back to him.

Ms. L, a single nurse with one son, cut off communication with a gentleman who seemed to be playing games. She really liked him, but I told her she had to stop texting and calling, and she did. One shocking morning, he came calling. She called me, so surprised!

Like I said, ladies, you don't need to sweat them—just sit back and wait! Follow my proven methods, especially if it's a man you want. Don't chase him because, eventually, he will come to you because men love a good mystery. You have control and now he's curious. Make sure you stay up to par so you will always be ready for a last-minute visit. You have to make him pursue you, because the man who legitimately pursues you wants you. So don't sweat or chase him!

Chapter 13:
Be Happy to
Hear from Him

When he does call you, remain cheerful and happy to hear from him. Never ask him why he hasn't called you! Keep the conversation current, wherever it may lead. Let him know you are just wonderful and you aren't angry because he took too long to call. Then ask him how he is doing.

Don't ever let a man think because he doesn't call you on a regular basis that you're sad about it. Girl, please! Keep it moving. Remember, you have a life. You look good, and you're accomplishing all of the things you want out of life. To be honest, at this point, you couldn't care less why he hasn't called because you actually are **wonderful**. He'd better hope you know who *he* is when he picks up the phone to dial your seven digits.

I have a gentleman friend who had not called me for a while. The last time we had talked, he said he was watching television and would call me back. Well, he didn't. A week went by. I called him and didn't get an answer, so I deleted his number everywhere I had it and moved on. Then, to my surprise, he called wishing me a happy new year, proclaiming that he missed me. I was flattered. He was a retired lieutenant colonel in the U.S. Army and lived in a mansion. I was happy to hear from him.

Chapter 14: Do Something Out of the Ordinary

If you are seeing a man, you have to do something in his life to leave an impact on his memory because bachelors have plenty of female friends. You want to stand out from the rest. For example, when visiting him, do something spontaneous in the winter like show up at his door wearing a fur coat and his favorite color lingerie, high heels, smelling fresh and sensuous. When he opens the door, open your coat with, "Surprise, baby!" Put a rose behind your back and reveal it by saying, "This is for you, baby." Wear just a raincoat in the rain. Wear no panties in the summer.

Do different things that you know will turn him on. Buy him birthday and Christmas gifts, or a gift just because you want to show him he means a lot to you. I know this works from experience.

I can't stress enough how important it is to

always be sexy, look and smell good, and say good things to him. He will want your company because your presence will put his mind at ease. You just might turn him from a bachelor to your husband. Your mental and physical upkeep must remain intact in order to get and keep a trustworthy, caring mate. Remember, every man loves a well-kept woman.

Chapter 15: Show Your Strength as a Woman

Be strong and brave enough to leave him if you have to. Please don't tolerate disrespect. You don't have to! If he doesn't treat you right, by all means, please leave him alone because there's another man who will treat you like a queen. If you stay and continue to accept mistreatment, you will never know or be able to experience something better.

Staying busy will assist you in getting past the sorrow of your loss and moving forward to bigger and brighter pastures. By putting yourself first and upholding a level of confidence that no one can bring down, you can and will move on.

Take time out of your busy schedule to pamper yourself. A day at the spa, dinner and a movie with a girlfriend or relative, a visit to the beauty shop, or something as simple as a Calgon candlelight bath with a glass of wine will do the trick. Focus on what's important to you and what makes you happy. Concentration on self-worth and building strength from within will be to your benefit in the long run as opposed to consuming your confused mind with an impossible "man mission."

Beauty comes from within and the rest takes care of itself. If you should run into this man, who wasn't right for you from the start, and you're looking good, smelling good, and sounding good, he won't be able to do anything but realize his loss!

The heart is soft most of the time and using the heart for your brain will be your downfall. Your soft spot will make it difficult to leave him alone. Yes, it hurts when he doesn't respond to text messages or doesn't return your calls. However, the relationship couldn't have been important to him if he was willing to abandon it that easily. Grin and bear it because this too will pass. You must be strong and endure through this difficult time. It is hard when your heart is in it *and* he knows you have feelings for him.

If he isn't treating you the way you deserve to be treated, give him a taste of his own medicine. Instead of answering to his every beck and call; duplicate his actions and don't respond. When and if you answer, tell him you're busy and you will get back with him, then don't! Let him see how it feels because, believe me, if he's calling or texting, he wants you. He will come back correct or move on—either way, you're better off!

It isn't a good feeling when your heart is into him, and he's playing games or is in denial of his true feelings for you. Either way, you don't have time for that. Life is too short. Show him that you don't need a man to complete you, and you can live without him.

I was in a short relationship with a gentleman who didn't want a commitment but wanted to keep seeing me. We continued to see each other for two years. Then I said I couldn't do it anymore because he should know by now if he wanted to be committed. I told him I was done. A week later, he made a cameo appearance at my job, and I wasn't there at the time he came. I don't know if he expected me to call, but I kept it moving.

After four weeks, I realized I had left some personal belongings at his place, so I contacted him to retrieve them. He kept making himself unavailable to me, so I took it upon myself to get out there to get my things. I called first. He didn't answer. This was after I saw that both of his cars were there. Then I rang the doorbell. After two attempts, he finally answered the door. He invited me in and closed the door behind me. I asked him to please hurry to get my belongings because my car was running and I had to go. He didn't bring all of my things, but I still left his place like a lady. I can still see his face and hear in his voice how upset he was. I couldn't care less. Keep it moving ladies; know your self-worth.

One other thing to keep in mind, ladies, is this: When we were born, there was no man attached to us. You can survive without him. Give him a chance to miss you. Cut off all communication so that he sees you mean business. Sometimes you may have to tell him to leave you alone, but show him you can do it. Even if you love him, let him go. You might want to hold on; you're no different than any other woman. A man is the same as any man in the world. Cut him off!

He is going to do one or the other—come back correct or move on. Let him go—not yourself! Keep it moving, ladies, and with a smile. Leave your heart open to fall in love again.

Do everything in your power to leave him alone. You have no control over him reaching out to you. This is something I personally went through. I cut off all communication with a gentleman with whom I was involved because I was in love with him and he didn't seem to care. I had to do what I had to do, so I left him alone in every way, form, and fashion. Every two or three weeks, he would contact me in some small way. I would always respond to him because I was still in love with him, but I still did everything in my power to leave him alone.

You can change your phone number or do what you have to do to move on. Being in love is a good thing, but you can also be sick in love as if you have the flu. Do what you have to do to get well. Love is grand with the right man, when he loves you back, and cares that you love him. Love is a good thing, and if a human being knows that you personally love them and they don't care— please move on. Real love is rare and is not promised.

Chapter 16:
Be Charming
(Keep Your
Game Tight)

Always try to be in a positive state of mind. Never be down in the dumps about a man. Don't let his actions affect your true and real personality. Learn to smile all the time. Give compliments and be sweet. Even a soft, gentle touch is a way to express love and kindness. A man enjoys it when a gorgeous, charming woman touches him. It catches his attention and alerts him that you are acknowledging him. A real man loves a confident woman. It shows you have stability and strength, and that you love yourself.

Chapter 7 refers to acceptable ways to stroke his ego. Mention that his scent is arousing, his intelligence motivates and inspires you, or compliment his eyes and deep dimples—whatever it is that you like about him should be made known to him. I promise you, he will love it. He will remain a friend, especially if you're a well-kept woman. Men love receiving compliments from gorgeous women because it shows you have security and aren't stuck on yourself.

Again, if you follow my proven methods, you will have a fan club of men who will call you just to see how you are doing, or even some that are ready to take you off the market. I have been married twice and have had at least five proposals since my last marriage, so it works. Be charming and, more importantly, always be yourself. Men love it!

Chapter 17:
Never Let Him
Get You Down

I can't stress enough that you should not let a man's actions get you out-of-whack. Out-of-whack meaning your daily routine or normal schedule shouldn't be interrupted due to heartache that he may have caused.

Losing sleep, not eating or overeating, missing work or being late for work is unacceptable. Don't let their negativity rub off on you because as the saying goes, 'Misery loves company.' Negativity manifests itself, so try everything in your power to stay cheerful. The things he chooses to do should never get your spirits down. Keep your head up and shake it off.

I have had male friends who think they are God's gift to women. They think they have women wrapped around their fingers. They think can say and do anything, and their women will still be there for them. Apparently, they've been dealing with a lot of females who tolerate nonsense. Don't fall into that same category. Choose to be cherished and cared about; nothing less. You deserve better, and there are good men out there. But you must first be a good woman to be selected by a good man.

Chapter 18:
Flirt with
Your Eyes

If you see a man to whom you're attracted, try flirting with your eyes. Don't say anything though. Smile and make it apparent that you're checking him out, but wait on him to say something to you. He will, if you follow my methods. Keep your best look on, be charming, smell fresh, and continue to be sexy. Even if he's married, he'll say something to you. However, before exchanging those alluring eye glances, check for a wedding ring to avoid unnecessary drama. Nothing could be worse than being the other woman.

All attention isn't good attention, even though I get it all the time from men everywhere I go—men at gas stations, church, work, parking lots, banks, grocery stores, etc. I tell you this from experience. I try to meet a certain standard everywhere I go. I see men all the time looking and doing double takes. They always say something like, "You're beautiful," gorgeous, sexy, etc. I flirt with my eyes. It's fun and I enjoy the extra attention. Try it, ladies. I dare you to look your best, experiment with flirty eyes, and watch men flock like pigeons to bread. Practice one day and see what happens!

Chapter 19:
Never Change
Who You Are

Never change who you are for a man! If you are in a committed relationship, yes, you need to compromise sometimes. But **don't** change your inner self to appease a man. You are unique, so love who you are and be **you**. When it all boils down, you have to live with yourself before anybody else; so please don't change who you are unless it is to better **yourself**.

There is nothing wrong with self-analysis. We all should evaluate our inconsistencies and downfalls in order to stay on our best game. However, when a man continuously finds fault in everything you do, it may be necessary to check *his* creditability as a compatible person for you. If you've done all you can, and he still isn't happy, proudly take your bow and exit.

Chapter 20: Maintain Your Independence

Ladies, please maintain your independence in your relationships. Always stand your ground, defend yourself, and stand up for yourself. Have your own everything. And I mean everything! Hold on to your own job, career, home, car, money, and your own opinion. Stay positive and continue to gain as much knowledge as you can because knowledge is power.

Love yourself at all times. I can't stress how important this is. Independence is part of your identity, so maintain it! My father always told me when I was young to take care of business— TCB! I thank him for this advice because it paid off. I am so independent! My bank account has my name as the account holder, so when I write a check, it's my signature that's inscribed when making purchases.

Something as simple as hanging a picture on a wall, or even as dirty as changing the tire on your vehicle, should always be achievable. This is because you've trained yourself not to depend on any human, who could possibly let you down. Let us not forget what's more important than any material or monetary items. We must take care of ourselves.

Once that special soul mate enters your life, he won't allow you to handle the difficult tasks, but at least you'll know, without a shadow of a doubt, that there is nothing you can't accomplish on your own. Make no mistake—if he's willing to take care of you, please don't turn him down. It is truly a wonderful thing to have a man love and care enough to make it his business to take care of you.

Closing Remarks

In closing my treatise on love and relationships, I want to emphasize that you should love yourself at all costs! You're worth it! Never let yourself go, with or without him, because in the end, all you have is you! This can be accomplished if you remain strong and follow my proven methods based on my experiences.

I have even had females who have given me compliments. My friend LaShawn states, "Thank you for inspiring me and showing that there is no age limit to making your dreams come true. With a focused heart and mind, and God on your side, you can do all things, even the impossible. Thank you for being an inspiration in my life."

Ruby, another friend writes, "In search of love and harmony, the book *With or Without* is a great tool to acknowledge your true self and full of recipes to find that special soul that completes yourself. Bravo!"

Ladies, take my advice and never let yourself go. Please have confidence in yourself. Be strong. Learn as much as you can in life. Be a jack-of-all-trades.

Writing this book is one of my many accomplishments. Life is good, and it's what you, as an individual, make of it.

I am the Harriet Tubman on love and relationships. If you follow me, you will not get caught up. You will be free from unnecessary heartache. Harriet Tubman was a slave who **freed herself** then led other slaves to freedom. She led them to safe houses and barnyards in the back of horse–drawn carriages covered with potato sacks, all the way to freedom. The twenty chapters in this book are my way of leading you to freedom from unnecessary mishaps.

I have the same mindset as Harriet Tubman. She had the desire to be free. She figured out a way and shared it with others who also wanted to be free. I was inspired by being tired of seeing women go through so much to get or keep a man that they would put up with anything. It's not that serious. Be free and enjoy your life, with or without him.

Book Inspiration

There were several books that inspired me on my journey to becoming a successful author. I would like to share them with you:

- *The Holy Bible*

- *How to Be an Irresistible Woman,* by E. E. Kelly

- *Getting to "I Do" (The Secret to Doing Relationships Right)* by Dr. Patricia Allen and Sandra Harmon

- *Words of Wisdom: Daily Affirmations of Faith,* by Rev Run

Choose to love yourself. Be happy, protect your heart, and love people. People are what make the world go around. Be kind, speak when out in public, open the door for the elderly, respect all people, especially your elders, and respect yourself.

You are special. Don't let anybody tell you differently. A peaceful life begins with a peaceful mind. I know that life has many challenges. Life IS a challenge itself. Be strong and you will be all right. LOVE YOURSELF at all costs. I love you, ladies!

Angela Reid

♥ Yourself